MAKING TIME FOR YOURSELF

A GUIDE TO SELF-CARE AND SELF-COMPASSION

DR. JAGADEESH PILLAI

Made with ❤ on the Notion Press Platform
www.notionpress.com

|| Dedicated to all wisdom seekers around the world ||

ᑭᑭᑭ

Contents

Contents

Prayer

**"Om Bhadram Karnebhih Shrunuyaama
DevaahBhadram Pashyemaakshabhiryajatraah
SthirairangaistushtuvaamsastanoobhihVyashema
Devahitam YadaayuhSwasti Na Indro
VridhashravaahSwasti Nah Pooshaa
VishwavedaahSwasti Nastaarkshyo ArishtanemihSwasti
No Brihaspatir DadhaatuOm Shantih, Shantih, Shantih"**

The literal meaning of this mantra is: OM. O Gods! Let us hear auspicious words from our ears. O reverent Gods! Let us behold propitious visions from our eyes, let our organs and body be stable, healthy, and strong. Let us do that which is pleasing to the gods in the life span allotted to us. May Indra, inscribed in the scriptures, bring us fortune! May Pushan, the knower of the world, grant us prosperity! May Trakshya, who vanquishes enemies, bestow us with blessings! May Brihaspati bring us success!
OM Peace, Peace, Peace.

About The Author

Dr. Jagadeesh Pillai is a renowned Guinness World Record holder, writer, and researcher hailing from Varanasi, also known as the abode of Lord Shiva. With a Ph.D. in Vedic Science and a range of creative ideas and achievements, he is a true polymath. He is the author of more than 100 books including Research Publications. Although his roots can be traced back to Kerala, the people of Varanasi hold him in high regard and affectionately consider him one of their own.

In 1998, Dr. Pillai was offered a job at Banaras Hindu University, but he left the position after only two months to pursue greater goals in life. He believed that in order to study Indian scriptures and engage in other creative endeavours, he needed to retire from the daily grind of working solely for money at a young age.

He started an export business from scratch, using the knowledge he had gained from a previous job in the industry. His intelligence and unique approach to business led to great success in a short period of time, earning him more in just a decade and a half than he would have in a lifetime working in a government job. Upon the passing of Dr. APJ Abdul Kalam, Dr. Pillai decided to leave the business and dedicate himself to reading, studying, researching, and experimenting.

During his tenure in the export business, Dr. Pillai traveled to over 16 countries, gaining valuable insight and experiencing the world and life in detail.

Dr. Pillai has achieved four Guinness World Records in the following subjects:

"Script to Screen" - In this record, Dr. Pillai produced and directed an animation film within the shortest time possible, breaking the previous record set by Canadians. He has also received numerous national and international awards and recognitions for this achievement.

Longest Line of Postcards - For this record, Dr. Pillai created a line of 16,300 postcards on the occasion of the 163rd anniversary of Indian Postal Day. The event also included a questionnaire about the Indian flag.

Largest Poster Awareness Campaign - Dr. Pillai designed an awareness campaign on the subject of "Beti Bachao - Beti Padhao" (Save the Girl Child - Educate the Girl Child) to achieve this record.

Largest Envelope - In tribute to the Indian Prime Minister's "Make in India" initiative, Dr. Pillai created a 4000 square meter envelope using waste paper to achieve this record.

Attempted - **70000 Candles on a 210 kg Cake** - To celebrate the 70th Indian Independence Day, Dr. Pillai attempted to light 70,000 candles on a 210 kg cake, which was recorded in World Records India.

Attempted - **Documentary on Dhamek Stupa of Sarnath in 17 Languages** - Dr. Pillai attempted to create a documentary on the Dhamek Stupa of Sarnath, dubbing it in 17 different languages. The result of this attempt is currently awaiting confirmation from the Guinness World Records.

Dr. Pillai is skilled in teaching the Bhagavad Gita, a Hindu scripture, and is popular among young people. He has helped many young people improve their lives through his motivational teachings.

In addition to teaching, he has composed and sung numerous Sanskrit Bhajans and patriotic songs.

He has also written and directed several short films and documentaries for awareness campaigns, and has volunteered with the police in both UP and Kerala to spread awareness about various issues through videos and photography.

Incredibly, he has produced and directed over 100 documentaries about the city of Varanasi, all on his own.

He has also helped and guided more than 25 boys and girls to achieve world records through creative and innovative methods. He is a multifaceted person who uses his intellect and the blessings given to him by God to excel in various areas. He is both a teacher and a student, always learning and teaching, and is able to master any subject he comes across.

He is a selfless social activist and motivational speaker who has overcome struggles and failures to become a successful and enthusiastic individual with a rich life experience.

In addition to his work with the Bhagavad Gita, he is also an efficient Tarot card reader, Astro-Vastu consultant, and a talented singer and composer. He has sung the entire Ram Charita Manas and Bhagavad Gita in his own compositions, and has sung the phrase "Lokah Samastha Sukhino Bhavantu" in 50 different languages. He is currently working on a detailed and scientific study of Vedas, Upanishads, Puranas, and the Bhagavad Gita. He has also composed and sung the Hanuman Chalisa and Gayatri Mantra in 108 and 1008 different compositions, respectively.

Awards - Four Times Guinness World Records, Winner of Mahatma Gandhi Vishwa Shanti Puraskar, Mahatma Gandhi Global Peace Ambassador, Kashi Ratna Award, Dr. APJ Abdul Kalam Motivational Person of the Year 2017, Mother Teresa Award, Indira Gandhi Priyadarshini Award, Bharat Vikas Ratna Award, Udyog Ratna Award, Vigyan Prasar Award, Poorvanchal Ratn Samman.

Preface

Welcome to "Making Time for Yourself: A Guide to Self-Care and Self-Compassion." The fast-paced and demanding world we live in can often leave us feeling overwhelmed, exhausted, and stressed. It's easy to prioritize work, responsibilities, and the needs of others, but neglecting our own well-being can have serious consequences.

Self-care and self-compassion are essential for promoting overall well-being, yet many of us struggle to make time for ourselves. This book is designed to help you understand the importance of self-care and self-compassion, and provide practical tools and techniques to incorporate them into your daily routine.

This guide covers various aspects of self-care and self-compassion, from taking stock of your needs to setting healthy goals and seeking support. You will learn about different self-care activities, such as mindfulness, gratitude, and connecting with nature, and how to make them a regular part of your life. The book also explores the concept of self-compassion and provides techniques to cultivate self-kindness, reduce self-criticism, and promote emotional resilience.

Whether you're new to self-care and self-compassion or looking to deepen your existing practices, this book provides a comprehensive and practical guide to making time for yourself. By taking care of yourself and being kind to yourself, you can better manage stress, improve your physical and mental health, and live a more fulfilling life.

So, take a deep breath, make yourself comfortable, and let's get started on your self-care and self-compassion journey. Your well-being and happiness are worth it.

ONE
Understanding Self-Care

Self-care refers to the actions and habits individuals undertake to promote their physical, mental, and emotional well-being. It encompasses a range of activities, from exercising regularly and eating a balanced diet to engaging in self-reflection and taking time for leisure activities.

Self-care is essential to a healthy, balanced life. It helps you manage stress, prevent burnout, and improve your overall quality of life. Additionally, when you prioritize your own well-being, you are better equipped to help others and navigate life's challenges.

However, despite its importance, self-care is often overlooked in our fast-paced, over-scheduled lives. We may put the needs of others before our own, or believe that taking care of ourselves is selfish. This couldn't be further from the truth. Self-care is a form of self-compassion, a way of being kind and understanding to ourselves.

There are many different forms of self-care, and what works best for one person may not work for another. Some common self-care activities include:

Exercise and physical activity

Eating a balanced diet and drinking enough water

Getting enough sleep

Connecting with friends and family

Taking breaks and engaging in leisure activities

Practicing mindfulness and meditation

Seeking support from mental health professionals

It's important to remember that self-care is a personal journey, and what works for one person may not work for another. The key is to experiment and find what works best for you.

In conclusion, understanding self-care is the first step to making time for yourself and prioritizing your well-being. By embracing self-care, you can improve your overall health and happiness, and become more resilient in the face of life's challenges.

"Self-care is not selfish, it's essential."

TWO

Taking Stock of Your Needs

Self-care is about taking care of your own physical, emotional, and mental well-being. To practice effective self-care, it's important to understand what your specific needs are and how best to meet them.

Here are some steps to help you take stock of your needs:

Assess your physical, emotional, and mental health: Take a moment to reflect on how you're feeling physically, emotionally, and mentally. Are you feeling stressed, burnt out, or overwhelmed? Are you experiencing physical discomfort or pain? Understanding your current state can help you prioritize self-care activities that will have the greatest impact.

Identify your stressors: What are the sources of stress in your life? Knowing what triggers your stress can help you develop strategies to manage it more effectively.

Evaluate your current self-care practices: What self-care activities do you currently engage in? Are they effective in reducing stress and promoting well-being? If not, it may be time to try new activities.

Set realistic goals: What self-care activities would you like to prioritize in your life? Make sure your goals are realistic and achievable, given your current lifestyle and circumstances.

By taking stock of your needs, you can develop a personalized self-care plan that works best for you. Remember that self-care is an ongoing process, and it's important to regularly reassess your needs and make adjustments as needed.

In conclusion, taking stock of your needs is an essential step in the self-care journey. By understanding what your needs are, you can prioritize self-care activities that will have the greatest impact on your physical, emotional, and mental well-being.

"Prioritizing yourself is not a luxury, it's a necessity."

THREE

PRIORITIZING YOUR TIME

Self-care often takes a back seat in our busy lives, but making time for yourself is essential to your physical, emotional, and mental well-being. In order to prioritize your time for self-care, it's important to assess your current schedule and make adjustments as needed.

Here are some steps to help you prioritize your time for self-care:

Schedule self-care activities: Treat self-care as a non-negotiable appointment in your schedule. Set aside specific times each week for self-care activities, and make them a priority just like any other appointment.

Be mindful of your commitments: Take a close look at your calendar and assess how much time you are committing to work, social events, and other obligations. Are there areas where you can reduce your commitments or delegate tasks to others?

Say "no" to non-essential commitments: It's okay to decline invitations or requests if they don't align with your priorities or well-being.

Learn to delegate: Don't be afraid to delegate tasks or responsibilities to others. This will free up more time for self-care and reduce your stress levels.

Make time for self-care in small increments: If you have a busy schedule, try incorporating self-care into your daily routine in small increments. Take a few deep breaths, go for a quick walk, or practice a few minutes of mindfulness.

By prioritizing your time for self-care, you can reduce stress, prevent burnout, and improve your overall well-being. Remember that self-care is not a luxury, but a necessity, and it's important to make it a priority in your life.

In conclusion, prioritizing your time for self-care is a crucial step in your self-care journey. By scheduling self-care activities, reducing non-essential commitments, and making time for self-care in small increments, you can improve your physical, emotional, and mental well-being and live a more fulfilling life.

"Take care of your body, it's the only place you have to live."

FOUR

Exploring Your Values

Your values are the beliefs, principles, and standards that guide your life and shape your decisions. Understanding your values can be an important tool in promoting self-care and self-compassion.

Here are some steps to help you explore your values:

Reflect on what's important to you: Take some time to think about what values are most important to you. Are your values aligned with your daily actions and decisions?

Identify areas of conflict: Are there any values that are in conflict with each other? This can be a source of stress and tension in your life.

Prioritize your values: Once you have identified your values, prioritize them based on their importance to you. This can help you make more mindful decisions in line with your values.

Make changes in alignment with your values: Take a close look at your daily habits and routines. Are there areas where you can make changes to align with your values? This could involve making changes in your work, relationships, or self-care practices.

Re-evaluate your values regularly: Your values can evolve and change over time. It's important to regularly re-evaluate your values and make adjustments as needed.

By exploring your values, you can better understand what is important to you and make more mindful decisions in line with your values. This can lead to greater happiness, fulfillment, and a more meaningful life.

In conclusion, exploring your values is an important aspect of self-care and self-compassion. By reflecting on what's important to you, prioritizing your values, and making changes in alignment with your values, you can live a more fulfilling life and promote your overall well-being.

"Self-compassion is giving yourself the same kindness and understanding you would give to a good friend."

♡♡♡

FIVE

Creating Boundaries

Boundaries are the physical, emotional, and psychological limits we set for ourselves to maintain our well-being and protect our time, energy, and resources. Establishing healthy boundaries is an important aspect of self-care and self-compassion.

Here are some steps to help you create healthy boundaries:

Identify your limits: Take some time to think about what limits you need to set in your life to protect your well-being. This could involve setting boundaries with work, relationships, or other commitments.

Communicate your boundaries: Clearly communicate your boundaries to others. This can be done through assertive communication, setting clear expectations, and saying "no" when necessary.

Stick to your boundaries: Once you have established your boundaries, it's important to stick to them. This may require saying "no" to others and saying "yes" to yourself.

Take responsibility for your boundaries: It's important to take responsibility for your own boundaries and not rely on others to enforce them for you.

Re-evaluate your boundaries regularly: Your needs and boundaries may change over time. It's important to regularly re-evaluate your boundaries and make adjustments as needed.

By creating healthy boundaries, you can protect your time, energy, and resources and promote your physical, emotional, and mental well-being. This can lead to greater happiness, fulfillment, and a more meaningful life.

In conclusion, creating healthy boundaries is an important aspect of self-care and self-compassion. By identifying your limits, communicating your boundaries, sticking to your boundaries, and regularly re-evaluating your boundaries, you can better protect your well-being and live a more fulfilling life.

"Your mental and emotional health is just as important as your physical health."

SIX

GUILT-FREE HOBBIES

Hobbies are a great way to relax, recharge, and pursue interests outside of work and other obligations. However, many people feel guilty when they take time for themselves and engage in hobbies, feeling that they should always be working or fulfilling responsibilities.

Here are some steps to help you pursue hobbies without guilt:

Identify your hobbies: Take some time to think about what activities bring you joy and relaxation. This could be anything from reading, painting, playing an instrument, to cooking, or gardening.

Make time for your hobbies: Schedule time for your hobbies into your weekly routine. This could be a set time each week or simply setting aside time each day for a specific activity.

Let go of guilt: Remind yourself that taking time for yourself and pursuing hobbies is important for your overall well-being. Let go of any guilt you may feel and embrace the positive benefits of engaging in these activities.

Share your hobbies with others: Engaging in hobbies with others can be a great way to build connections and create a supportive community. Share your hobbies with friends and family or join a club or group centered around your interests.

Make it a priority: Prioritize your hobbies and make time for them just as you would for any other important obligation or responsibility.

By pursuing hobbies without guilt, you can relax, recharge, and pursue interests that bring you joy. This can lead to greater happiness, fulfillment, and a more meaningful life.

In conclusion, engaging in hobbies without guilt is an important aspect of self-care and self-compassion. By identifying your hobbies, making time for them, letting go of guilt, sharing your hobbies with others, and making them a priority, you can better promote your overall well-being and live a more fulfilling life.

"Making time for yourself is not an indulgence, it's an investment in your well-being."

SEVEN

Setting Healthy Goals

Goals can provide direction and motivation in life, but they can also cause stress and anxiety if they are unrealistic or unattainable. Setting healthy goals is an important aspect of self-care and self-compassion.

Here are some steps to help you set healthy goals:

Identify what you want to achieve: Take some time to think about what you want to achieve in various aspects of your life, such as personal, professional, financial, or health-related.

Set realistic and achievable goals: Make sure that your goals are realistic and achievable. This may require breaking down larger goals into smaller, manageable steps.

Focus on progress, not perfection: Instead of focusing on perfection, focus on progress. Celebrate small wins and progress along the way.

Prioritize self-care: Make self-care a priority as you work towards your goals. Taking care of yourself should always come before reaching your goals.

Be flexible: Life can be unpredictable, and it's important to be flexible and adapt to change. Be open to adjusting your goals as needed and recognizing when it's time to let go of certain goals.

By setting healthy goals, you can achieve what you want in life while also taking care of your well-being. This can lead to greater happiness, fulfillment, and a more meaningful life.

In conclusion, setting healthy goals is an important aspect of self-care and self-compassion. By identifying what you want to achieve, setting realistic and achievable goals, focusing on progress, prioritizing self-care, and being flexible, you can better promote your overall well-being and live a more fulfilling life.

"Be kind to yourself, you're doing the best you can."

EIGHT

MAKING ROOM FOR FUN

Having fun is an important aspect of self-care and self-compassion, but it can often get neglected in the midst of work and other responsibilities. Making room for fun can help improve overall well-being, reduce stress, and bring joy and excitement to life.

Here are some steps to help you make room for fun:

Identify your sense of fun: Take some time to think about what activities bring you joy and excitement. This could be anything from outdoor activities, visiting museums, attending concerts, to trying new hobbies.

Schedule time for fun: Make time for fun a priority by scheduling it into your weekly routine. This could be a set time each week or simply setting aside time each day for a specific activity.

Let go of stress and worries: When engaging in fun

activities, try to let go of stress and worries. Embrace the moment and fully immerse yourself in the experience.

Share your fun with others: Engaging in fun activities with others can be a great way to build connections and create a supportive community. Share your sense of fun with friends and family.

Make it a priority: Prioritize fun and make time for it just as you would for any other important obligation or responsibility.

By making room for fun, you can improve overall well-being, reduce stress, and bring joy and excitement to life.

In conclusion, making room for fun is an important aspect of self-care and self-compassion. By identifying your sense of fun, scheduling time for it, letting go of stress and worries, sharing your fun with others, and making it a priority, you can better promote your overall well-being and live a more fulfilling life.

"Mindfulness is the key to unlocking a happier and healthier life."

NINE

LEARNING TO RECHARGE

In today's fast-paced world, it's important to take breaks and recharge to maintain physical and emotional well-being. Recharging can come in many forms, such as taking a nap, engaging in a hobby, spending time with loved ones, or simply taking a walk in nature.

Here are some steps to help you learn to recharge:

Identify what recharges you: Take some time to reflect on what activities and experiences help you recharge and reduce stress. This could be different for everyone, so it's important to find what works best for you.

Set aside time for recharge: Make sure to set aside time for recharging each day, week, or month. This could be a dedicated time for self-care or simply taking breaks throughout the day.

Make it a priority: Treat recharging as a priority, just as you would with any other important obligation or responsibility. This may require adjusting your schedule or saying no to other commitments.

Experiment with different methods: Try different methods of recharging and see what works best for you. This could include physical activities, spending time in nature, or engaging in a creative pursuit.

Practice mindfulness: Practice mindfulness while recharging. Focus on the present moment and allow yourself to fully relax and rejuvenate.

By learning to recharge, you can maintain physical and emotional well-being, reduce stress, and improve overall happiness.

In conclusion, learning to recharge is an important aspect of self-care and self-compassion. By identifying what recharges you, setting aside time for recharge, making it a priority, experimenting with different methods, and practicing mindfulness, you can better promote your overall well-being and live a more fulfilling life.

"Gratitude is the fertilizer for a happy life."

ჶჶჶ

TEN

PRACTICING SELF-COMPASSION

Self-compassion is the act of treating yourself with kindness and understanding, rather than self-criticism or self-judgment. It involves recognizing and accepting your own imperfections and failures, and treating yourself with the same compassion and understanding that you would offer to others.

Here are some steps to help you practice self-compassion:

Recognize self-criticism: Start by becoming aware of when you engage in self-criticism or self-judgment. This could be thoughts related to your appearance, performance, or worth.

Reframe negative thoughts: When you recognize self-criticism, try to reframe these thoughts in a kind and understanding way. Instead of saying "I'm such a failure," try saying "I made a mistake and that's okay."

Be kind to yourself: Treat yourself with kindness and understanding, just as you would with a good friend. This could involve giving yourself compliments, practicing self-care, or doing something that brings you joy.

Practice mindfulness: Practice mindfulness to become more aware of your thoughts and emotions. This can help you recognize negative thoughts and respond to them with compassion and understanding.

Surround yourself with positive influences: Surround yourself with people who support and encourage you. This could be friends, family, or a support group.

By practicing self-compassion, you can reduce self-criticism and negative self-talk, increase overall happiness and well-being, and build resilience in the face of challenges and setbacks.

In conclusion, practicing self-compassion is an important aspect of self-care and self-compassion. By recognizing self-criticism, reframing negative thoughts, being kind to yourself, practicing mindfulness, and surrounding yourself with positive influences, you can better promote your overall well-being and live a more fulfilling life.

"Invest in yourself, it will pay off in every aspect of your life."

♡♡♡

ELEVEN

Integrating Self-Care into Your Life

Self-care and self-compassion are essential for overall well-being, but they can be difficult to make a habit. Integrating self-care into your daily routine is crucial to ensure it becomes a regular part of your life.

Here are some tips for integrating self-care into your life:

Make a plan: Set aside specific times each day or week for self-care activities, such as exercise, meditation, or reading a book.

Find what works for you: Experiment with different self-care activities to find what works best for you, and make sure they align with your values and goals.

Make it a priority: Make self-care a priority in your life by scheduling it into your daily routine and putting it ahead of other commitments.

Make it enjoyable: Make self-care enjoyable by incorporating activities you enjoy, such as a favorite hobby or spending time in nature.

Be consistent: Be consistent in your self-care practices to make it a habit and ensure long-term benefits.

By integrating self-care into your life, you can ensure it becomes a regular part of your routine and promote overall well-being.

In conclusion, integrating self-care into your life is crucial for overall well-being. By making a plan, finding what works for you, making it a priority, making it enjoyable, and being consistent, you can better promote your overall well-being and live a more fulfilling life.

♡♡♡

"Nature has a way of healing what's broken within us."

TWELVE

CONNECTING TO NATURE

Nature has a profound impact on our physical and emotional well-being. Spending time in nature can reduce stress, improve mood, and promote overall health and happiness.

Here are some ways to help you connect with nature:

Get outside: Make a conscious effort to spend time outside, whether it be for a walk in the park, a hike in the mountains, or simply sitting in a garden.

Engage your senses: Take the time to fully engage your senses while in nature. This could include observing the beauty of the surroundings, listening to birdsong, or smelling the fragrance of flowers.

Unplug: Disconnect from technology and devices, and fully immerse yourself in the natural environment.

Practice mindfulness: Practice mindfulness while in nature, focusing on the present moment and the beauty and wonder of the surroundings.

Connect with nature regularly: Make connecting with nature a regular part of your routine, whether it be once a day, once a week, or once a month.

By connecting with nature, you can reduce stress, improve mood, and promote overall well-being.

In conclusion, connecting to nature is an important aspect of self-care and self-compassion. By getting outside, engaging your senses, unplugging, practicing mindfulness, and connecting with nature regularly, you can better promote your overall well-being and live a more fulfilling life.

♡♡♡

"A healthy dose of self-care can work wonders for your soul."

THIRTEEN

CULTIVATING MINDFULNESS

Mindfulness is the practice of being present in the moment and paying attention to thoughts, feelings, and sensations without judgment. It can help reduce stress, improve mental health, and promote overall well-being.

Here are some ways to help cultivate mindfulness in your daily life:

Practice daily meditation: Start with a daily mindfulness meditation practice, such as deep breathing exercises or guided meditations.

Live in the present: Practice being present in the moment and focusing on the here and now, rather than dwelling on the past or worrying about the future.

Engage in mindful activities: Engage in activities that encourage mindfulness, such as yoga, tai chi, or gardening.

Be aware of your thoughts: Become aware of your thoughts, feelings, and sensations, and observe them without judgment.

Practice gratitude: Practice gratitude by focusing on the positive aspects of your life, and expressing gratitude for them.

By cultivating mindfulness, you can reduce stress, improve mental health, and promote overall well-being.

In conclusion, mindfulness is an important aspect of self-care and self-compassion. By practicing daily meditation, living in the present, engaging in mindful activities, being aware of your thoughts, and practicing gratitude, you can better promote your overall well-being and live a more fulfilling life.

"When we practice self-care, we give ourselves the gift of a lifetime."

FOURTEEN

MAKING SPACE FOR GRATITUDE

Gratitude is the practice of being thankful and appreciative for what we have in our lives, no matter how big or small. It can help improve mental health, increase happiness, and promote overall well-being.

Here are some ways to make space for gratitude in your daily life:

Keep a gratitude journal: Write down things you are thankful for each day, no matter how small.

Practice daily gratitude: Make a conscious effort to focus on the things you are grateful for each day, such as a warm bed, good health, or a loving family.

Express gratitude to others: Express gratitude to others by thanking them for their support and kindness.

Focus on the positive: Rather than dwelling on the negative, focus on the positive aspects of your life.

Engage in acts of kindness: Engage in acts of kindness, such as volunteering or helping a neighbor, to increase feelings of gratitude.

By making space for gratitude in your daily life, you can improve mental health, increase happiness, and promote overall well-being.

In conclusion, gratitude is an important aspect of self-care and self-compassion. By keeping a gratitude journal, practicing daily gratitude, expressing gratitude to others, focusing on the positive, and engaging in acts of kindness, you can better promote your overall well-being and live a more fulfilling life.

"Self-compassion helps us build resilience and overcome challenges."

ꨄꨄꨄ

FIFTEEN

SEEKING SUPPORT

Self-care and self-compassion can be challenging to maintain, especially when life gets busy or stressful. Seeking support from others can help you stay on track and maintain your well-being.

Here are some ways to seek support in your self-care and self-compassion journey:

Reach out to friends and family: Reach out to loved ones for support, whether it be for a chat, a hug, or a helping hand.

Join a support group: Join a support group, either in person or online, where you can connect with others who are going through similar experiences.

Work with a therapist: Consider working with a therapist who can provide guidance and support in your self-care and self-compassion journey.

Seek out community resources: Take advantage of community resources, such as free classes or workshops, to help you maintain your self-care and self-compassion practices.

Surround yourself with positive people: Surround yourself with positive and supportive people who will encourage and motivate you on your journey.

By seeking support from others, you can stay on track and maintain your self-care and self-compassion practices, even when life gets busy or stressful.

In conclusion, seeking support is an important aspect of self-care and self-compassion. By reaching out to friends and family, joining a support group, working with a therapist, seeking out community resources, and surrounding yourself with positive people, you can better promote your overall well-being and live a more fulfilling life.

"Making time for yourself is not a selfish act, it's self-preservation."

♡♡♡

Other Books Of The Author

1. The Moments When I Met God
2. Kashiyile Theertha Pathangal
3. GURU GYAN VANI
4. Abhiprerak Gita
5. ASSI SE JAIN GHAT TAK
6. Hopelessness of Arjuna
7. The Soul and It's True Nature
8. Sense of Action (Karma)
9. Action through Wisdom
10. Action through Wisdom
11. THEORY AND PRACTICAL OF EVERY ACTION
12. LOGICAL UNDERSTANDING OF THE SUPREME
13. THE IMPERISHABLE SUPREME
14. Yatra Nishadraj se Hanuman Ghat Tak
15. Yatra Karnatak Ghat se Raja Ghat Tak
16. Yatra Pandey Ghat se Prayagraj Ghat Tak
17. Yatra Ranjendra Prasad Ghat se Dattatreya Ghat Tak
18. YaatraSindhiya Ghat se Gwaliar Ghat Tak
19. Yatra Mangala Gauri Ghat se Hanuman Gadhi Ghat Tak
20. Yatra Gaay Ghat Se Nishad Ghat Tak
21. MAA GANGA, GHATEN EVM UTSAV
22. Ganga Arti Dev Deepavali evam Any Utsav
23. Potentials of Digitalized India
24. VEDIC CONSCIOUSNESS
25. A Brief Introduction to Vedic Science
26. Kashi ke Barah Jyotirling
27. IMPACT OF MOTIVATION
28. Let's have a Milky Way Journey
29. Color Therapy in a Nutshell

30. Rigveda in a Nutshell
31. Yajurveda in a Nutshell
32. Samveda in a Nutshell
33. Atharva Veda in a Nutshell
34. Ayushman Bhava - Ayurveda
35. Srimad Bhagavad Gita and Upanishad Connection
36. Srimad Bhagavad Gita - an attempt to summarize each chapter.
37. Facts and Impact of Nakshatra
38. Astro Gems - NAVARATNA
39. Ekadashi - A Concise Overview
40. A Concise View of Hanuman Chalisa
41. Inspirational Gita
42. Nakshatraranyam
43. Summary of 18 Mahapuranas
44. Synopsis of 18 Upa Puranas
45. Rigvediya Upanishads
46. Shukla Yajurvediya Upanishads
47. Krishna Yajurvediya Upanishads
48. Samavediya Upanishads
49. Atharvavediya Upanishads
50. The Seven Great Sages
51. From Rocket Scientist to President Dr. APJ Abdul Kalam
52. The Visionary's Voice - Quotes of Dr. APJ Abdul Kalam
53. The Wisdom of Swami Vivekananda: Insights and Inspiration from a Legendary Spiritual Teacher
54. Ayurvedic Remedies from the Garden
55. Sages and Seers
56. Rising Strong – Motivational Stories of Women
57. Beyond Flames -Mystery stories of Funeral Ghat Manikarnika
58. The Origins of Tulsi: A Look at the Mythological Roots of the Plant"

59. The Holistic Cow: A Look at the Physical, Spiritual, and Cultural Importance of Cows in India
60. Arts of Healing
61. Exploring the Divine
62. Understanding Five Elements
63. The Etymology of Ram
64. Symbols of India
65. Voice of Change (About Speeches of Great Men)
66. She Speaks (About Speeches of Great Women)
67. Patriotism on Celluloid – Brief About Patriotic Films
68. The Music of Motivation: A Brief Guide to Inspirational Film Songs
69. **Unlocking the Secrets of the Dashopanishads**
70. A Cultural Mosaic
71. Ancient Traditions, Modern Minds
72. Ecos of Ancient Wisdom
73. Beneath the Surface
74. From Temples to Ashrams
75. Sages of the Subcontinent
76. The Art of Healling (Ayurveda, Yoga & Naturopathy)
77. Indian Kitchen
78. The Festivals of India
79. The Indian Epics Retold
80. The Power of Mantras
81. The Indian River Ganges
82. The Indian Architecture
83. Rites of Passage
84. The Indian Silk Road
85. The Indian Literature
86. The Indian Villages
87. The Indian Folks & Crafts
88. The Way of Buddha
89. The Ramayan of Tulsidas

90. Astrological Remedies
91. The Secret Power of Motivation
92. Secret of Developing your Inner Strength
93. The Secret Path to Motivation
94. The Art and Secret of Positive Thinking
95. The Secrets of Practicing Ethical Living
96. Indian Art and Painting
97. The Indian Herbalism
98. Bharatanatyam to Kathak
99. Exploring India's Astrological Remedies
100. The Indian Festival of Flowers
101. Indian Handicrafts
102. The Splashes of Joy – India's Colour Festival
103. The Indian Science of Astrology
104. The Indian Mythology
105. Path to Enlightenment
106. The Indian Spirituality for Children
107. Aromas of India
108. The Secrets of Healthy Relationships
109. Ancestral Ties
110. The Indian Street Food
111. Discovering America
112. The Indian Textile
113. Listening to Motivational Speeches
114. Taste of India
115. A Cultural Journey through Indian Nuptials
116. Motivational Quote for Change
117. Secret Strategies for Making Money
118. Secrets to Cultivate a Positive Mindset
119. A Tapestry of Cultures: Exploring India from Kashmir to Kanyakumari
120. Achieving Your Dreams with Resilience: Secret Strategies for Overcoming Obstacles

121. Innovative Startups - 25 Startup Ideas to Spark Your Business Creativity
122. Export Management: Strategies for Global Success
123. Exporting from India - A Step by Step Guide
124. Finance Fundamentals: Mastering Financial Management for Business Success
125. Global Growth Strategies for International Business Development
126. Marketing Mastery: Unlocking the Secrets of Modern Marketing
127. Operations Mastery: Managing the Flow of Value in Business
128. Strategic Business Management: Navigating the Modern Business Landscape
129. Human Resource Management Strategies for Building and Managing a High Performance Team
130. The Indian Landscapes and Nature: An Exploration Of India's Natural Beauty And Diversity
131. The Indian Street Performances: A Cultural Exploration of India's Street Performances
132. Affirming Your Self-Worth: Strategies for Achieving Emotional Wellbeing
133. Cultivating Self-Discipline: Secrets Methods for Achieving Your Goals
134. Embracing Change: Strategies for Adapting to Life's Challenges
135. Embracing Your Uniqueness: Secret Strategies for Living an Authentic Life
136. Finding Motivation in Despondency: Coping with Difficult Times

Contact

DR. JAGADEESH PILLAI

MBA & PhD in Vedic Science

Four Times Guinness World Record Holder

Winner of Mahatma Gandhi Vishwa Shanti Puraskar and
Global Peace Ambassador

Gemology, Astro & Vastu Consultant - Spiritual Counselor

Consultant for designing World Record Ideas

Efficient Tarot Card Reader

9839093003

myrichindia@gmail.com

drjagadeeshpillai@facebook

drjagadeeshpillai@instagram
jagadeeshpillai@youtube

www. JAGADEESHPILLAI.com

Contact

|| LOKAHA SAMASTHAHA SUKHINO BHAVANTU ||

Printed by Libri Plureos GmbH in Hamburg,
Germany